Albert takes to the sky

The Adventures of Albert Mouse
Book Three

James Hywel

OINK

First published by Oink Books 2022

Copyright © 2022 by James Hywel

All rights reserved. No part of this publication may be reproduced, stored or transmitted in any form or by any means, electronic, mechanical, photocopying, recording, scanning, or otherwise without written permission from the publisher. It is illegal to copy this book, post it to a website, or distribute it by any other means without permission.

This novel is entirely a work of fiction. The names, characters and incidents portrayed in it are the work of the author's imagination. Any resemblance to actual persons, living or dead, events or localities is entirely coincidental.

James Hywel asserts the moral right to be identified as the author of this work.

James Hywel has no responsibility for the persistence or accuracy of URLs for external or third-party Internet Websites referred to in this publication and does not guarantee that any content on such Websites is, or will remain, accurate or appropriate.

Designations used by companies to distinguish their products are often claimed as trademarks. All brand names and product names used in this book and on its cover are trade names, service marks, trademarks and registered trademarks of their respective owners. The publishers and the book are not associated with any product or vendor mentioned in this book. None of the companies referenced within the book has endorsed the book.

Although the publisher and the author have made every effort to ensure that the information in this book was correct at press time, the publisher and the author assume no responsibility for errors, including grammar and spelling mistakes. They will endeavour to rectify these in future editions.

Written for

Morgan & Josie

and

Mr Spike

Albert Books

The mouse who wanted to see the world

Albert and the smuggler Mickey Mustard

Albert takes to the sky

Albert and the runaway train

Albert buys a boat

Albert learns to swim

Albert and the Newcomen Engine

Chapter 1

As usual, the sun was shining and it was another glorious day in Dartmouth. What was not so usual was the fact that Albert was not sitting at his bedroom window.

Instead, he was lying in the garden under the shade of a small tree staring up at the sky.

He had been there for quite a while, just watching the clouds slowly drift by.

"I do like living here," the little mouse eventually said to himself with a contented sigh.

His peace was suddenly disturbed by a voice from the front door. It was his sister Millie.

"What are you doing, Albert?" she asked.

"Nothing, just watching the clouds and relaxing," said her brother.

Millie turned and ran back into the house.

"Mum, Albert's being lazy in the garden," she said to her mother.

"You should worry less about what your brother is doing and more about not telling tales on people," said Mrs Mouse. "Anyway, knowing Albert he is probably thinking about something."

Albert was indeed thinking about something, for at that very moment he saw a large multicoloured balloon appear over the horizon and it was heading in his direction.

"Oh wow, it's a balloon!" said Albert excitedly, jumping to his feet.

As he watched the balloon get closer and closer he realised that it had a small basket suspended underneath it and inside the basket were people.

Albert quickly ran into the house.

"Mum, come and look at this balloon in the sky," he said, pulling at his Mum's hand.

"Ok, ok, calm down!" said his mother as she put her knitting on the coffee table and got to her feet.

"See!" said Albert, pointing to the large balloon that was now almost overhead.

"It is, indeed," said his mother. "Girls, come and see."

Soon Dorothy and Millie had joined Albert and his mother in the garden and they were all gazing up at the balloon.

The occupants of the basket were waving at people in the streets who had also stopped to look up.

"Wow, can you imagine what it must be like to be up there?" said Albert.

"You wouldn't get me in one of those things for all the cheese in...," Mrs Mouse paused, as she thought about where would have the most cheese.

"Well, wherever, but it's definitely not for me," said Mrs Mouse.

"I'd go in one of those if I had the chance," said Albert.

"Would you really?" asked Millie, looking at her brother. "Wouldn't you be scared of falling out?"

"Oh no, not me, and, anyway, I suspect it's perfectly safe," said her brother, even though the highest place he had ever been was his bedroom window sill.

By now the balloon had drifted out of sight, so Dorothy, Millie and Mrs Mouse went back into the house.

Albert walked back to his spot under the tree to imagine what it would be like to fly in the air.

Chapter 2

As Albert folded his arms behind his head and tried to imagine flying in the air, there was a flutter of wings and a large gull landed next to him on the grass.

"Morning," said Big Tony.

"Did you see the balloon?" asked Albert looking at his friend.

"I did. They are a liability, clogging up the sky. Shouldn't be allowed if you ask me," said the gull.

"I think they are quite amazing. I'd love to go in one," said Albert.

"You wouldn't get me in one of those death traps," said the gull.

"Death-trap?" asked the little mouse, looking worried.

"I reckon so. From my experience, flying isn't easy, you know, it takes years of practice," said Big Tony.

"Oh, I thought it was easy?" said the little mouse.

"Easy? Are you kidding? It's a delicate exercise that can all go wrong in the blink of an eye," said Big Tony.

"Really? Then what, do you crash?" asked Albert.

"Yes, or worse," said the gull.

"Wow, I had no idea. I've watched you open your wings and glide down from my roof lots of times and you make it look so easy," said Albert.

"That's 'cause I'm an expert. No, in my opinion, if you didn't come into this world from an egg, then you have no right to be in the air," said Big Tony.

Albert thought about this for a few moments.

"Crocodiles come from eggs, but they don't fly," said Albert.

The gull hadn't considered this.

"Ok, well you should only be allowed to fly if you have feathers then," huffed the gull.

"Chickens have feathers and they can't fly for toffee," giggled Albert.

"True, but then look at them. I mean, they're not exactly the brightest of birds are they?" chuckled the gull.

"True," agreed Albert.

Just then Albert's mother appeared at the front door.

"I thought I heard your voice, Tony, would you like a cheese sandwich?" she asked.

"Er, no thank you, Mrs M., I've just had a rather large bag of chips and half a burger."

"What about you, Albert?" she asked.

"No thanks, Mum, I'm fine," said the little mouse.

Once Mrs Mouse had gone back into the house, Albert and Big Tony continued their conversation.

"Like I said, if you don't lay eggs, have feathers and you're a chicken, then stay on the ground and leave the flying to us experts," said the gull.

"You're right, but I'd still like to try it once," sighed Albert.

Then an idea suddenly came to him.

"I know, why don't you give me a ride on your back? We wouldn't have to go far or very high, maybe just to the roof and back. What do you think?" said Albert. "Tony...?"

But the gull had nodded off in the sunshine and hadn't heard a word Albert had said.

The little mouse closed his eyes and soon he had fallen asleep too.

Chapter 3

From the window Albert's mother looked out into the garden where her son and the gull were asleep on the lawn.

She smiled to herself.

"I don't know. It seems like it was only last week that they were Dartmouth's famous crime-fighting duo, and now look at them. Both fast asleep, under the tree," she said.

In the distance, Mrs Mouse heard the sound of an ice-cream van playing its familiar tune over the loudspeaker.

Big Tony jumped, opened his eyes and looked around.

"Albert, I've got to go," said the gull as he gave a large yawn and stretched his wings.

"Ok, Big Tony. Maybe I'll see you later?" said Albert, sitting up.

The gull took a few steps and launched himself into the air.

"Hmmm, he does make it look so easy," thought Albert.

The little mouse stood up and took a few steps and flapped his arms, trying to imagine being able to fly. He then went inside the house.

"Mum, I may have that cheese sandwich now, if that's ok?" he said.

"I thought you might, so I made you one. It's in the fridge," said his mother.

Albert collected his sandwich and went outside to sit and eat it on the step.

As he ate the sandwich his mind kept going back to the balloon he'd seen floating over the house. He remembered what Big Tony had said, but could flying really be that difficult?

Once he had finished his sandwich, he wiped his hands on his trousers and stood up.

"Mum, I'm just going to the bookshop. I'll be back in a moment," he called.

"Ok dear, please be careful," replied his mother from the kitchen.

Albert walked down the path, then squeezed under the gate and headed for the bookshop.

"Oh, hello Albert. Nice to see you again. What can I do for you today?" said the lady behind the counter in the bookshop.

"Hello, Mrs Saunders. I wonder if you have any books on flying?" asked Albert.

"Ah, so I expect you saw the balloon then?" she said.

"Yes, I did and I want to find out a bit more about them if I can," said the mouse.

"Ok, well, let's see. I think we have a few books here," said Mrs Saunders, walking to one of the shelves. "Ah, yes, here we are, 'The history of flight'. This one has lots of great illustrations too."

"That's perfect," said Albert.

"Now, will you be ok with that or do you want me to help you take it home?"

"No, I'll be fine. I'll bring it back tomorrow," said the little mouse.

"Right you are. Well, it's nice to see you again, Albert. Give my love to your mother."

"I will," said Albert as he climbed down the steps and hurried back along the pavement.

He then squeezed back under the gate and sat down in the shade of the tree to read his book.

Chapter 4

Albert turned page after page, reading about planes, helicopters and even parachutes. Finally, he got to the section on balloons and was so absorbed in the book that he didn't hear his sister Millie coming out of the house.

"What are you reading about?" she asked, looking over his shoulder.

"Nothing!" said Albert, snapping the book shut quickly.

"Yes, you are, I saw you. What's it about?" asked his sister.

"It's just about planes and stuff, nothing that would be of interest to you," said Albert, keeping the book firmly shut.

"Where did you get it from?" Millie asked.

"From the bookshop, obviously," said Albert, wishing his sister would go back inside so he could get back to his reading.

"Mum, Albert has stolen a book from the bookshop!" Millie shouted as she ran back inside the house.

Albert sighed, then opened the book again and began to read about balloons.

In the kitchen, Millie was still trying to convince her mother that Albert had stolen the book.

"But he has! He's reading it in the garden," insisted Millie.

"Will you please stop that! Mrs Saunders at the bookshop very kindly allows Albert to borrow books sometimes," said Mrs Mouse firmly.

"Yes, but do remember he tore that map out of one of her books before?" added Millie.

"I know. But if you remember he gave Mrs Saunders the money for the book from his reward money for catching Mickey Mustard," said her mother.

Millie huffed and sat down on the sofa with her arms folded.

Back in the garden Albert had finished reading about balloons and was now even more excited than before. He closed the book and ran inside.

"Mum, did you know that the first balloon flight was on the twenty-first of November 1783?" said Albert

"I have to admit that I did not know that," said Mrs Mouse.

"Yes! And it was in a place called France. I'm not really sure where that is but never mind. The important thing is that the balloon went five hundred feet into the air and travelled for five and a half miles!"

"That sounds very impressive."

"It is impressive. Anyway, I'm off to the bookshop to return the book and ask Mrs Saunders some questions," said Albert.

"Oh, Albert, please don't disturb her. She has a shop to run, you know?"

"It's fine. She said I can drop in any time I like. Anyway, I'll only be there a few minutes, because I have some very important things to do," said the little mouse.

Albert's mother sighed and hoped Mrs Saunders wouldn't be too cross with Albert.

Chapter 5

Albert ran out of the house, squeezed under the garden gate and headed to the bookshop.

"Hello Mrs Saunders," said the little mouse as he hopped up the steps into the shop.

"Hello Albert. Was the book helpful?"

"Yes, it's a very interesting book, but I just wondered if I can keep it for a few more days?" asked the little mouse.

"Of course, Albert. You can bring it back whenever you're finished with it," asked Mrs Saunders.

"Thank you. I was just wondering if you knew where I could buy some balloons?"

"Balloons?" said Mrs Saunders, sounding surprised. "I think we may have a packet here on one of the stands….yes, here we are. Is it someone's birthday?"

"No, I'm going to build a balloon just like the one I've seen in the book but don't tell anyone, especially not Big Tony," said Albert, gently tapping the side of his nose with his finger.

"Your secret's safe with me, Albert," said Mrs Saunders.

"How much do I owe you for the balloons?" asked the mouse.

"Oh, don't worry about that, Albert, you keep your money."

"Wow, thank you so much!" said Albert. "Remember, not a word to anyone."

"My lips are sealed," said Mrs Saunders.

With that, Albert jumped down the steps and ran home.

His mother was sweeping the step as Albert squeezed back under the gate.

"You were quick," she said.

"I just wanted to ask Mrs Saunders if I can keep the book for a few more days and she said yes."

His mother noticed the small packet that her son had under his arm.

"And what's that you have?" she asked.

Albert looked around to make sure Big Tony wasn't around.

"It's just equipment for something that I am building, but please don't tell anyone. It's a secret," said Albert.

"Hmmm, just as long as you're not building some kind of flying machine?" asked his mother, looking at Albert over her glasses.

Albert laughed nervously.

"Don't be silly, Mum, how would I know how to build a flying machine?" he said, picking up his book and running upstairs to his bedroom.

Chapter 6

In his bedroom, Albert opened his bedside cupboard and searched for something.

"Ah, there it is!" he said, holding up the cardboard notice that had the words 'TOP SECRET WORK' - Keep Out!' in big letters on it. He'd used this sign when he was trying to capture the smuggler Mickey Mustard.

Albert opened his door and hung the sign on the door handle and then closed the door again.

He then climbed onto his bed and opened the book to the page about balloon flight.

"What are you reading?" asked a voice at the window, causing Albert to jump.

"Nothing," said the little mouse, closing the book quickly.

The gull looked suspiciously at Albert.

"Well, you were reading something," said Big Tony.

"Erm, it's just a book on cooking. It's my mother's birthday soon and

I've decided to bake her a cake," said the little mouse nervously.

"Birthday you say?" asked the gull, trying to look at the cover of the book.

"Yes, look I have some birthday balloons here," said Albert.

"So, why has it got a plane on the cover?" asked Big Tony.

"That's because you have to use plain flour when you make a cake. Did you not know that?" asked the little mouse.

"Hmmm, no I didn't," admitted Big Tony. "So, are you having a party and everything?"

"Oh yes, but numbers are very limited. In fact, it's a very small party, just the family," said Albert.

The gull looked very disappointed.

"But I'll obviously save you a piece of cake."

This seemed to cheer the gull up a little because Big Tony did like cake.

"Thanks, well I'll leave you your cake recipe. I'm off to the quay to look for an ice-cream," said Big Tony, and with that, he opened his wings, gently leapt into the air and was gone.

"Phew, that was lucky! Big Tony nearly saw what I was doing," said Albert to himself as he opened the book again.

Chapter 7

Outside Albert's door, Dorothy and Millie were lying on the floor trying to look under the door to see what their brother was doing that was so top secret.

"Can you see him?" asked Millie, in a whisper.

"No. He's not on the window sill," replied Dorothy quietly.

As she strained her eye, she suddenly caught a glimpse of something twitching and moving from side to side. It was the tip of her brother's tail.

"Wait, I see him. He's laid on the bed, but I can't see what he's doing," said Dorothy.

The two girls had been so busy looking under the door, that they hadn't heard their mother coming up the stairs.

"And what do you both think you're doing?" asked Mrs Mouse.

Both girls hurriedly got to their feet.

"We were just trying to see ....," began Millie, but Dorothy quickly placed her hand over her sister's mouth.

"Nothing," said Dorothy.

Their mother folded her arms.

"Well, it appears to me that you were spying on your brother and that is very rude, especially when you can see he doesn't want to be disturbed. Now, downstairs, the both of you and if I catch you looking under his door again, there will be trouble."

Dorothy and Millie went downstairs to play in the garden.

Mrs Mouse then knocked on Albert's bedroom door.

"Yes, who is it?" asked Albert.

"Just me, is it ok if I come in?" asked his mother.

"Yes," said the little mouse as he quickly shut the book again.

"I just wanted to see if your Top Secret stuff is going well?" asked his mother.

"I haven't really started yet, I'm still researching," said Albert.

"Is Big Tony helping you with whatever this new top-secret project is? I only ask because I thought I heard his voice."

"No, he's not. He was here, but he's just left to go and get himself an ice-cream. If I'm honest this is so secret that not even Big Tony knows anything about it," said Albert.

"Right, well that means it must be very important stuff indeed. As long as it's not dangerous?" asked Mrs Mouse.

Albert didn't answer.

"Would you like me to bring you a glass of milk and a cheese sandwich?"

"Oh, yes please," smiled the little mouse.

Chapter 8

After Albert had eaten his sandwich and finished his milk, he placed the empty plate and glass outside his door and then climbed back onto his bed.

He took another look at the wonderful illustration of the hot-air balloon.

"Right, I think this should be easy enough," he said, opening the packet of balloons that Mrs Saunders had given him.

There was a huge selection of colours but Albert decided to use the red one because it matched his bow-tie.

The little mouse took several deep breaths, then held the balloon up to his mouth and blew as hard as he could. The flat balloon didn't inflate, in fact, it hardly moved.

Albert took several more deep breaths and blew into the balloon as hard as he could.

Suddenly the room started to go dark and Albert saw several stars appear. He also started to feel a little dizzy. Soon the room brightened up, but he could still see the stars.

"Hmmm, this flying business is harder than it looks," he said, taking a rest to catch his breath.

Albert knew that if he couldn't even inflate one balloon then his top-secret plan may be finished before it had even got off the ground, so he thought for a moment.

"Of course!" he said eventually with a big smile on his face, picked up the balloon again and jumped off the bed.

He then opened his door and went downstairs.

"Mum, I'm off to the bookshop," said Albert as he passed the lounge door where his mother was reading the newspaper.

"Oh, Albert, you can't keep disturbing Mrs Saunders, she has a shop to run," said his mother.

There was no reply from her son.

"Albert?" she called.

But Albert didn't answer, because by now he was squeezing himself back under the garden gate on his way to see Mrs Saunders.

Chapter 9

The little mouse hopped up the steps to the bookshop and went inside.

"Sorry to disturb you, Mrs Saunders, but I wonder if you can help me?" he asked.

"Of course, Albert, what seems to be the problem?"

"I can't blow up the balloon for my top secret project, I think I'm too small. Actually, I've been trying so hard that everything went dark and I started to see stars. So, I wondered if you could do it for me?" Albert asked, handing the balloon to the lady.

Mrs Saunders took a large deep breath and the balloon started to inflate.

"How's that?" she asked as she tied the end of the balloon in a knot and handed it back to Albert.

"Wow, that's perfect. Thank you so much!" said the little mouse excitedly.

Albert jumped down the steps and went home.

When he got to the gate he suddenly realised that he wouldn't be able to squeeze back under with the balloon.

"Oh, this is a problem that I hadn't quite anticipated," he said to himself.

So the little mouse sat down on the pavement to make a plan.

"There's nothing for it," he said. "I'll just have to climb up over the wall."

Placing the knotted end of the balloon in his mouth, Albert scrambled up and over the wall and ran into the house.

"Where are you going with that?" asked his mother.

"With what?"

"The balloon?" said his mother.

"It's part of my top-secret project so I can't really tell you anything about it right now," said Albert, rushing upstairs to his bedroom and slamming the door behind him.

Albert opened his bedside cupboard and found his ball of string and some scissors. He wasn't sure how long to have the string but he thought it should be quite long, so he cut a length of string and tied it to the bottom of the balloon. Then holding the end of the string, he climbed up onto the window sill.

The little mouse held onto the end of the string as tightly as he could and looked down into the garden.

"Gosh, it does look a long way down from here," he said and stepped back onto his window sill. "Maybe I should let a test pilot try it first?"

Albert looked round the room. There, in the corner, sat Albert's teddy bear.

"Teddy, I now promote you to Chief Test Pilot," announced Albert, jumping back down onto the floor and going across to his teddy.

"Are you ready for this dangerous mission?" Albert asked, but Teddy seemed to be frozen with fear because he didn't answer.

"Don't worry. I've done all the safety checks and if all goes to plan, you should have a soft landing in the flowerbed," said Albert, as he picked up his bear.

Albert tied the end of the string around Teddy's middle and then climbed back onto the windowsill.

The three of them stood there - Teddy, the balloon and Albert. The bear looked down to the garden below and then looked at Albert.

"Don't worry, it's perfectly safe. I just need to do a few pre-flight checks and then we can commence launch," said Albert.

"Balloon check. String check. All systems go! Are you ready?" he asked, looking at his bear.

The bear shook his head, but Albert had already started the countdown so there was no going back now.

"...four, three, two, one. Now remember to land in something soft, GO!" said Albert and he launched Teddy out of the window.

Chapter 10

Albert leaned out of the window and watched Teddy, suspended by the balloon, plummet to the ground.

"Head for the flowerbed! No, not there, the flowerbed!" shouted Albert, but Teddy obviously hadn't heard the instructions because he landed on the hard stone path, bouncing several times.

"Stay there! I'm coming!" shouted Albert, jumping down onto the floor and rushing downstairs.

"Mum, Albert's just thrown his Teddy Bear out of the window," shouted Dorothy.

Mrs Mouse got out of her chair and went to the door, just as Albert ran past her into the garden.

"Have you just thrown your bear out of the window?" she asked him.

"Yes, but he had a balloon. He's my test pilot. Anyway, I can't talk now. He's crash-landed into the garden and may be in need of medical attention," said Albert running down the steps to where Teddy lay, motionless.

"Teddy, are you ok? Talk to me," said Albert.

The bear looked stunned, but apart from that was unharmed.

"I think we might need a bigger balloon," said Albert, looking at his bear. "Or more balloons! Then we just need to make a few adjustments for the next flight."

"Next flight?" asked his mother, shaking her head and going back into the house.

Albert ran upstairs and picked up another balloon from the packet, then ran back to the bookshop.

"How is your Top Secret Mission going? I just saw Teddy leaping from the window into the garden," said Mrs Saunders.

"It's going well, but I think we need another balloon to carry Teddy's weight," said Albert.

Soon Mrs Saunders had blown up the blue balloon and handed it back to Albert.

"Thank you," he said, leaving the shop with the balloon and scrambling back up the wall into his garden.

Upstairs in his bedroom, Albert tied another piece of string to the second balloon and then again tied that around Teddy's waist.

By now a small group of people had gathered outside Albert's house and they all held their cameras ready for Teddy's second flight.

Albert gave them a wave and then turned to his teddy.

"Ready?" Albert asked.

The bear shook his head. He was still a bit bruised from the first flight, but he hoped that having two balloons would give him a softer landing, so he stood at the open window and closed his eyes.

"Balloons - check. Strings - check. All systems go! Stand by for the second test flight! Five, four, three, two, one, GO!" said Albert and he again launched Teddy out of the window.

The small crowd cheered as Teddy made his jump.

"Mum, Albert's just thrown his Teddy Bear out of the window again," shouted Dorothy.

"Yes, thank you, dear. I don't need to know every time it happens," said Mrs Mouse.

Chapter II

Albert again watched as his Teddy descended to the ground, only this time the speed was much slower, but the bear still bounced several times.

"Almost there," said Albert, as he took another balloon from the packet and ran downstairs.

The little mouse checked on the state of Teddy, who seemed ok, so Albert squeezed under the gate and went to see Mrs Saunders.

"Mum, Albert's just gone to the bookshop again!" shouted Dorothy.

Mrs Mouse sighed and carried on reading her newspaper.

"It seems Teddy had a better landing this time," said Mrs Saunders at the bookshop, taking the yellow balloon from Albert.

"Yes! I think three balloons will be just the job," said Albert.

"There you go," she said, handing the yellow balloon to Albert. "You'd better be careful, I think the wind is picking up."

"Thanks, I'll keep an eye on it for the next flight," said the little mouse and he again scrambled up and over the wall.

Albert picked up his bear and then ran back upstairs to his bedroom.

Soon, Teddy had three balloons attached tightly around his waist and was ready to take his third test flight.

Albert remembered what Mrs Saunders had said and licked his paw, then held it out of the window to check the wind direction.

"No wind. That's good," he said. "Right, are you ready?" asked Albert, looking at his bear.

The bear closed his eyes and again shook his head.

"Five, four, three, two, one, GO!" said Albert and he again launched Teddy out of the window.

The bear floated gently down to the ground and landed in the flowerbed.

"Hooray! A perfect landing!" cheered Albert.

The crowd were all cheering and clapping their hands. Even Mrs Saunders, who had been watching from the shop doorway, clapped her hands.

Albert felt very pleased with himself and ran downstairs.

"Mum, you should have seen that one, it was perfect!" said Albert excitedly as he ran into the garden to collect Teddy from under the white hydrangea bush.

Both he and Teddy bowed in front of the people who had gathered at the other side of the wall and posed for several photos.

Albert then went back into the house.

Chapter 12

Soon Albert appeared in his bedroom window again and waved to the growing crowd below who cheered and took photographs.

Albert then turned back and looked at Teddy, who looked reluctant to do another test flight.

"It's ok, Teddy, I think the test flights are over. Now it's my turn," he said.

The little mouse looked around the room.

"But what I need is a basket," he said.

Then in the corner of his bedroom, he saw his backpack.

"Or a harness!"

Albert then undid the balloon strings from Teddy's waist and attached them to his backpack. He checked that the knots were very tight.

"Right, safety first," he said to himself and placed the ball of string in the backpack. "I might need that if one of the strings breaks."

Albert then put the backpack over his shoulders.

Teddy looked very worried.

"It's fine, this is exactly the sort of thing the people with the parachutes are wearing in the book. Anyway, I can't disappoint my fans," said the little mouse as he stepped out onto the window ledge.

"Albert, Albert, Albert!" cheered the crowd of people.

Albert waved again, then licked his finger to check the wind direction.

"Perfect," he said.

Inside the house, Mrs Mouse could hear the crowd cheering and looked up from her newspaper.

"I really don't know why they are getting so excited about a teddy bear being thrown out of the window. I really liked it so much more when Albert wasn't famous," she sighed.

Soon the crowd began to count down from ten as Albert stood on the window ledge, holding onto the window frame.

"...... four, three, two, one, GO!" they shouted.

Albert let go of the window and held onto the straps of his backpack, then, with a leap, he launched himself off the window ledge.

Chapter 13

The little mouse had expected to drift slowly to the ground, but instead, a sudden gust of wind came out of nowhere and caught the three balloons lifting Albert upwards.

"Oops!" said Albert.

The crowd gasped in horror.

"Oh my goodness!" said Mrs Saunders at the bookshop, hardly able to believe her eyes.

Albert was powerless to do anything as he watched the crowd of people outside his house get smaller and smaller as he rose higher into the air.

"Mum, Albert's flying in the sky!" shouted Millie, who had been sitting in the garden with her sister.

"How many times have I told you not to tell tales about your brother," said Mrs Mouse.

"Millie's right, Mum, Albert's flying!" said Dorothy. "Come and see!"

Mrs Mouse put her newspaper down and walked into the garden.

"Look, there he is," said Dorothy, pointing to a small speck in the sky.

Mrs Mouse stared in disbelief.

"Are you sure that's Albert?" she asked. "Are you sure it's not his teddy?"

"No, there's his teddy in the window," said Millie, pointing to the worried-looking bear that was sitting on the window sill in Albert's bedroom.

"Oh no! Someone, please do something!" said Mrs Mouse.

The problem was that no one on the ground could help Albert, who was now floating off in the direction of Dartmouth Castle.

"I'll call the police, the fire brigade and the RNLI," said Mrs Saunders, running back into the bookshop.

Chapter 14

While Mrs Saunders was telephoning the emergency services, Albert was just passing over the small car park at the castle.

As he waved to a few people who had looked up to see as the three balloons approached, the little mouse noticed something.

Flying from a tall pole on one of the towers was a large white and red flag.

"Hmm, if I could just catch hold of that, then I might be able to untie the balloons and climb down the pole. Then I could get home," thought the mouse.

Albert knew that he would only get one chance at this so he kicked his legs trying to cause the balloons to head towards the flag.

"I think I'm getting there," said Albert, still kicking his legs.

The little mouse was right. He did appear to be heading for the flag and was now just a few feet away.

Just then the flag flapped in the wind and the end of it hit Albert in the face, so he immediately grabbed the material.

"Got it!" he said triumphantly and held on to the fabric as hard as he could.

The problem was that the flag was flapping around in the wind and so were his three balloons. All of a sudden, a strong wind shook the flag and the little mouse lost his grip.

"Oh no!"

Albert kicked his legs again trying to get back to the flag, but it was too late. The little mouse drifted further and further away from the flag and was now directly above Castle Cove.

A worried look came over Albert's face as he realised that he was now heading out to sea where Big Tony said the rest of the world was.

"This is not good. I didn't think this would happen or I would have packed some lunch," said the little mouse, remembering he had only had a cheese sandwich and a glass of milk for breakfast.

Chapter 15

Back at Higher Street, Mrs Saunders ran out of the shop and leaned over the garden wall.

"Mrs Mouse, the RNLI lifeboat has been launched and they are looking for Albert," she said.

"Well, I suppose that's a relief, but Albert's only small and there's a lot of sky and water out there," said Mrs Mouse, sounding panicked.

"Well, we need to be hopeful, and, anyway, Albert's not just any mouse, is he? I'm sure he is already planning something to get himself down," said Mrs Saunders reassuringly.

Back under the three balloons, Albert was not planning anything. He was looking at the town of Dartmouth getting further and further away. It dawned on him that this could be the end and he may never see home again.

"I love you, Mum," he sniffed and tears rolled down his cheeks. "I'm sorry I got myself into such a mess."

Just then the wind changed direction and the balloons swung

round and Albert was pushed towards Kingswear, on the other side of the estuary.

"Phew, that was lucky!" he said to himself, as he dried his eyes.

"I wish I'd read the part in the book that explained how to land a balloon," thought the little mouse.

Just then Albert saw an orange boat speeding down the estuary towards him. Albert politely waved at the men inside. Suddenly there was a loud voice coming through the air.

"Albert Mouse, this is the crew of the Dart Lifeboat. Please wave your arms if you can hear us."

Albert thought this was a strange request, but he wanted to be polite so he waved his arms up and down.

"Good. Now listen, we are here to rescue you. We need you to cut one of the balloons loose. This should allow you to descend into the water where we can pick you up. Do you understand?" asked the loud voice in the boat.

Albert looked up at the three balloons that were above his head and then looked down at the water below him. If he was honest he didn't really want to cut any of the balloons free. Neither did he want to land in the water. He may be Dartmouth's greatest explorer, but he couldn't swim.

"Er, no, it's alright, thank you. Do you have another plan?" shouted the mouse.

"Say again, we can't hear you," said the loud voice.

"N-O T-H-A-N-K Y-O-U!" shouted Albert as loud as he could, but the men in the boat couldn't hear him.

Chapter 16

At that moment Albert remembered the ball of string that he had put inside his backpack.

"Of course," he said.

Albert twisted his arm behind him and felt around inside the backpack.

"Got it!" he said.

The little mouse then tied the end of the string to one of the straps of the backpack.

Down in the orange boat, the man with the binoculars saw what Albert was doing and gave the order to the rest of the crew.

"Albert's going to drop a line down to us. Everyone get ready because we will only have one chance at this, so make sure one of us catches the string!" said the man.

The captain manoeuvred the orange boat under the balloons and everyone got ready.

Albert knew that this may be his only chance at rescue so he took a few deep breaths and then began to count down from five.

"Five, four, three, two, one."

Albert let go of the ball of string and watched it tumble through the air towards the waiting boat.

"Here it comes," said one of the men.

"Got it!" said another, as he caught the ball of string.

"Good catch!" shouted Albert.

"Ok, start to pull him down, but slowly. We don't want to snap the string," said the man with the binoculars.

Albert felt a gentle tug on the straps of his backpack as the men began to slowly pull on the string.

"Don't worry, Albert," said the loud voice. "We'll have you down in a few moments."

Albert held tightly onto the straps of his backpack.

The wind on the river started to pick up and Albert felt himself being bumped around against the tension of the string.

"Gently chaps, easy does it," said one of the crew in the boat.

Gradually Albert got closer and closer to the boat. He could see that one of the men had a large net on a stick and was holding it ready.

"Nearly there, chaps. Gently, gently," said the man again.

Albert was now just a few feet above the boat when there was a sudden gust of wind and the string snapped.

The man with the net jumped as high as he could and swished the net to try and catch Albert, but it was no good. The little mouse shot back up into the air.

Albert kicked his legs but it was now good. The wind was too strong and soon the balloons carried him across to the other side of the estuary and away from the boat.

"We did our best, but there is nothing we can do. Let's return to base," said the captain.

With that, the orange turned and headed back to the Lifeboat station, leaving Albert alone in the sky again.

Chapter 17

Albert watched as the orange boat disappeared up the river.

"Oh well," he said to himself as he drifted over the houses of Kingswear.

Albert looked down at the different coloured houses that lined the streets. There were blue ones, pink ones and even red ones. He wondered if any of his relatives lived in them, so waved just in case they did.

Suddenly there was a loud high-pitched whistle which gave Albert quite a shock.

Near the brightly painted houses, Albert saw a plume of smoke rise between the rooftops. The little mouse squinted his eyes and then he saw it.

It was a train and not just any train.

"Oh wow, it's a steam train!" said Albert excitedly.

Slowly Albert drifted over the station. He could see the lovely green steam train sitting on the platform and behind it were several brown carriages.

Some children, who were getting out of the carriage, had noticed the balloons in the sky and were pointing up at Albert.

Albert waved.

"Hello, welcome to Dartmouth. My name is Albert Mouse. You've probably heard of me," he shouted, but the children couldn't hear him.

Albert watched the smoke rise out of the train's chimney.

"When I get back home me and Big Tony will buy a ticket and take a ride on that train. It looks very exciting," the little mouse thought to himself.

Soon Albert had drifted past the station and past the painted houses. Now all he could see in front of him were green fields, lots of them that appeared to go on for miles and miles.

The little mouse had now forgotten about the steam train and was feeling sad and very alone again.

"I wish Big Tony was here," he said to himself, looking around, but there was no sign of his friend.

Albert began to cry again.

Chapter 18

At NO. 10, Mrs Mouse was getting more and more worried about her son.

"There, there," said Mrs Saunders. "I'm sure the emergency services will find him soon. And, anyway, Albert is a brave boy, so don't worry."

Big Tony, who had finished his ice-cream, came to see what all the commotion was and landed in the garden.

"What's all the excitement, Mrs M?" asked the gull.

"Oh, Big Tony, it's Albert. He's been carried away by a balloon," said Mrs Mouse.

"What, the one that passed over this morning?"

"No, it's a long story but he tied three balloons together and jumped out of his bedroom window. Then a gust of wind carried him away."

"I knew he was up to something," said Big Tony. "I did warn him about trying to fly. I said that if you didn't come into this world from an egg, then you have no right to be in the air."

"Crocodiles come from eggs, but they don't fly," said Dorothy.

"Dorothy, that's enough. Big Tony is right, if you haven't got wings you should stay on the ground," said her mother.

"Which way did he go?" asked the gull.

"That way I think," said Mrs Mouse pointing towards the castle.

"Right, leave this to me, I'll find him. By the way, what colours were the balloons?" asked Big Tony.

"Yellow, red and blue," said Dorothy.

"Got it," said the gull and in a few steps and a couple of flaps of his wings he was in the air and circling over the house looking for his friend.

Gradually Big Tony made larger and large circles in the air as he scanned the sky, then headed over to the castle.

"I do hope Big Tony can find him," said Albert's mother.

"Oh, I'm sure he will, Mrs Mouse. Big Tony can spot a pasty at a mile so if anyone can see Albert it's him," said Mrs Saunders. "Let me make you a cup of tea while we wait for news."

Chapter 19

It didn't take Big Tony long to reach the castle, but there was no sign of Albert.

Just then the gull noticed a torn red balloon in the branches of a tree near St Petrox Church.

"Oh no," said the gull, fearing the worst.

Big Tony flew across to the tree.

"Albert, Albert! Are you there?" he shouted, but there was no answer.

A small robin that had been sitting in a nearby hedge, flew across to the tree.

"Hey, Big Tony, are you looking for someone?" he asked.

"Yes, my friend - Albert. He's a small mouse about so big. He floated this way tied to three balloons," said the gull.

"Yes, I saw him. Came past here a few minutes ago. Crashed into that flag pole over there, before the wind carried off that way," said the robin.

"What, not out to sea?" asked the gull.

"Yes. I thought he was a goner, but, luckily for him, the wind changed," continued the robin.

"So, which way did he go then?"

"Back up the river. If you want my opinion, mice shouldn't be allowed in the air," said the robin and flew back to his hedge.

Big Tony opened his wings and launched himself back into the air. Just as he did he noticed a number of children at the small ice-cream kiosk.

"Note to self, I'll have to come back here later," he said, before heading back up the estuary in his search for Albert.

Chapter 20

High in the sky above the River Dart, Albert was still feeling sorry for himself and trying to come up with a plan to get back to earth when he heard another voice, only this time it wasn't from the men in the orange boat.

Albert looked round and there, flying alongside, was a large gull.

"Having fun, are we?" asked Big Tony.

"Big Tony! Am I glad to see you!" replied Albert, smiling from ear to ear. "Fun? No, not really. I seem to have got myself into a bit of a mess if I'm honest."

"A bit? I'd say you were in a big mess. As big as a man who has just stood in some dog poo," said Big Tony. "It's just a good job that the wind changed direction when it did, otherwise you would have ended up in America!"

"Yes, I must admit I was a bit worried for a moment as I passed the castle. I mean, I don't even speak American."

Just then Albert looked back at Dartmouth and noticed that a large crowd had gathered on the quayside, and there were also several police cars and a fire engine.

"Wow, look at all those police cars. Do you think Mickey Mustard is in trouble again?" asked Albert.

The gull glanced towards the quay.

"No, but I think you are," he said.

"Are they all there because of me?" asked Albert.

"Yes, and your mother isn't too happy either," said Big Tony.

"Oh dear," said Albert. "I should have listened to you this morning about flying being more difficult than it seems."

"It's too late now," said the gull.

"Is it really?" said the little mouse with a tear in his eye.

"Well, it would be if I hadn't come along to rescue you," said Big Tony.

"Really? Do you think you can?" said Albert, drying his eyes with his paw.

"Don't you worry my little friend. I'll get you home safe," said the gull. "But first I think I should go and tell your mother that you are ok and see if the police and fire engines can go home. I'll be back in a moment."

"Ok, but can you do me a favour?" asked Albert.

"Sure, I should have thought, you must be hungry. I'll bring you a bag of chips or half a pasty on the way back. What about a bacon, lettuce and tomato sandwich?" said the gull.

"No, it's not that, but it's very kind of you," said Albert.

"So, what is it?"

"Can you tell my Mum that I'm sorry?" said Albert.

"I think she knows that already," said the gull.

Albert gently nodded his head.

With that the gull turned and hurried back to Dartmouth, leaving Albert to think about all the trouble he had caused as he looked down at the sheep in the fields.

"I wonder if I'm more than five hundred feet about the ground?" Albert thought to himself.

Chapter 21

Big Tony soon arrived back at No. 10 Higher Street and was quite surprised by the enormous crowd that had now filled the street. They were all waiting for news of Albert. Even the TV reporters were there to cover the story.

The gull landed in the garden and walked over to Mrs Mouse.

"Oh, please tell me you've found Albert?" she said.

"I have. He's fine and there's nothing to worry about, but where have all these people come from?" asked the gull.

"As soon as they heard what had happened they just all arrived," said Mrs Mouse.

"Hi everyone, Big Tony has found Albert!" said Mrs Saunders, replaying the message to the waiting crowd.

There was a huge cheer.

"Where is he?" asked Mrs Mouse.

"Well, luckily for him, the wind changed direction just as he was about to head out to sea and he was blown back over to Kingswear. I managed to catch up with him. I've spoken to him and he is in good spirits. He is heading across the fields towards Brixham," said the gull.

"Oh no! What are we going to do?" asked Albert's mother looking quite upset.

"There, there, don't worry," said Big Tony. "I'm going to head back to him now to attempt a rescue. I'll have him back here before you can say 'chickens can't fly', so just try and stay calm."

"Hi everyone, Big Tony is going to attempt to save Albert," shouted

Mrs Saunders. "Three cheers for Big Tony!"

"Hip-hip-hooray, hooray, hooray!" cheered the crowd.

"Albert has missed his lunch, so he must be hungry. Let me quickly make him a cheese sandwich for you to take," said Mrs Mouse.

"It's ok, I did offer to bring him some food but he said he was fine. Anyway, I'd better get back to him."

Big Tony waved to the crowd and then launched himself into the air.

"Don't worry, Mum, Big Tony will bring Albert back," said Dorothy, who was now missing her brother.

"Yes, Mum, if anyone can save Albert it's Big Tony," said Millie.

Mrs Mouse took a hankie out of her pocket and blew her nose.

Chapter 22

Big Tony flew as fast as he could over the River Dart and across the fields.

He soon found Albert again.

"Am I glad to see you!" said the little mouse. "Is my Mum ok?"

"She's fine, but what we need to do now is burst those balloons," said the gull.

"What!" screamed Albert, holding tightly to the straps of his backpack.

"Relax, I'm just kidding," chuckled Big Tony.

"Phew, that's a relief," said Albert looking down at the fields that looked very small indeed.

"Right, I'm going to gently fly underneath you and I want you to catch hold of me and hold on tight. Ok?"

"I will try. Do you think this will work?" asked Albert.

"We'll soon find out," said the gull.

Slowly Big Tony swooped down below the little mouse until he was flying directly underneath Albert.

"Ready?" he shouted.

"Ready!" said Albert.

Gradually the gull started to come closer and closer to Albert's feet.

The little mouse reached down and grabbed two handfuls of feathers and held on.

"Well done, Albert," said the gull.

"Now what?" asked the mouse.

"Now I'm going to burst the balloons! Hold tight," said Big Tony.

With that, the gull reached his head round and pecked one of the balloons which instantly burst with a loud bang.

"Well done!" said Albert.

The gull then pecked the second balloon, then the third.

"Right, now pull on the strings and try to put the burst balloons in your backpack."

"Can't I just undo the strings and let them fall to the ground?" asked Albert.

"Certainly not!" exclaimed the gull. "Do you know how many animals and birds are killed by balloons each year?"

Albert shook his head.

"Well, a lot, and you were nearly added to that list," said the gull.

Albert pulled each of the strings in and pushed them and the burst balloons into his backpack.

"All done?" asked the gull.

"Yes. I'd really like to go home now if that's ok," said Albert.

"Right, hold on tight," said Big Tony.

The gull turned, flapped his wings and soon they were gliding gracefully back towards Dartmouth which was now a very long way away.

Chapter 23

In the lifeboat station, the boat crews were still watching the sky for any sign of Albert.

Suddenly one of the men saw Big Tony approaching with Albert on his back.

"Get on the radio, Big Tony has rescued Albert!" he shouted.

Another man picked up the handset that was on the desk and spoke into the mouthpiece.

"Albert is safe!" came the announcement.

In Higher Street, the crowds heard the cheering coming from the quayside.

"Albert's safe!" they shouted.

"Really, is it true?" asked Mrs Mouse.

"Yes, the RNLI station has just confirmed that Big Tony has rescued Albert and they are on their way here," said Mrs Saunders, giving Albert's mother a hug.

"Oh, thank goodness," cried Mrs Mouse.

Moments later the crowd could see Big Tony circling overhead with Albert on his back.

"Look Mum, there's Albert," said Dorothy.

Albert saw his mother and waved.

After circling a few times, Big Tony gently glided down and landed in the garden.

Albert jumped off the gull's back and waved to everyone, as he walked over to his mother.

"Oh Albert, I'm so glad you're safe," she said, giving a big hug.

"I was fine Mum, but I'm sorry I worried you so much," said Albert.

Dorothy and Millie then gave their brother a hug.

"We're glad you're safe," said Dorothy.

"Were you scared up there?" asked Millie.

"Me? No, I wasn't at all scared," said the little mouse.

"Albert, can we please have a few words?" asked the man from the TV company, holding a microphone in his hand.

The little mouse walked across to the news reporter.

"Albert, what does it feel like to be back on the ground?" asked the man.

"It's good to be home with my family," answered Albert.

"People are saying that this was your first flight, can you tell us what went wrong?"

"Yes, this was my first flight. Teddy had made several test flights and weather conditions were good, so I decided to attempt a flight myself. As I launched myself from my bedroom window a sudden gust of wind caught the balloons and carried me out to sea," said Albert. "Using my experience and flying skills I managed to steer the balloons back across the harbour."

"And that's where the RNLI Lifeboat tried to rescue you, is that correct?"

"You mean the men in the orange boat? Yes, as a safety measure I had put a ball of string in my backpack and threw that down to the waiting boat. Unfortunately, the weather conditions were extremely hazardous and a violent storm blew me from side to side, eventually snapping the string," said Albert.

"I see. And now I'd like to talk to Big Tony, who managed this daring rescue. Big Tony, was it dangerous out there?"

"Extremely. For a moment I thought the two of us were not going to be seen again. But thanks to Albert's dare-devil mid-air manoeuvres and my skilful flying, we are both here talking to you today," said the gull.

"One last question if I may. How will you be celebrating today after this heroic act?"

"I'll be having half a pasty, some chips and maybe an ice-cream," said Big Tony, remembering the kiosk he'd seen at the castle.

"And you, Albert?" asked the reporter.

"I'll be having a cheese sandwich with my family and then a long nap," said the little mouse.

The reporter then turned to the TV camera.

"Well, there you have it. Albert Mouse has been rescued by Big Tony in what many are calling the most death-defying mid-air rescue in the history of Dartmouth, possibly even in the whole of Devon. Now it's back to the studio."

Chapter 24

After their TV interview, Albert and Big Tony posed for photos and then signed some autographs.

Mrs Mouse went into the house and made a large pot of tea, while Dorothy and Millie made cheese sandwiches for everyone.

As the afternoon passed by, gradually the crowd of people slowly left and a quietness descended on No. 10 Higher Street.

"Well, that was quite a day," said Mrs Mouse.

"Yes, I'm sorry, Mum. I didn't mean to worry you as I did," said Albert, as he ate a sandwich.

"You're back now and that's all that matters. Hopefully, you've learnt an important lesson?" said his mother.

"I have, Mum, and the lesson is that if you didn't come into this world from an egg, don't have feathers or are a chicken then you shouldn't be flying in the air, isn't that right Big Tony?" giggled Albert.

"Exactly right. You should have listened to me this morning and then none of this would have happened," said the gull.

"Yes, but then just look at what an adventure I would have missed out on," said Albert.

His mother gave the little mouse a very disapproving look.

"Albert Mouse, I think you are officially grounded from now on. The highest place I ever want to see you is your bedroom window and no more balloons!"

"Yes, Mum," said Albert.

"And make sure you take that book back to Mrs Saunders," said his mother.

"Can I read it first?" asked Dorothy.

"No! We've had far too much excitement for one day," said Mrs Mouse.

For his brave rescue of Albert Mouse that day, Big Tony was given the 'Medal of the RNLI' at a ceremony at the Town Hall.

Sometimes even now, Big Tony sits on top of the Lifeboat station watching for people in distress. Although some less charitable people say he is just looking for someone who is not paying attention while eating their lunch on one of the nearby benches.

I hope you have enjoyed reading about
my adventures with
Big Tony.
If you come to Dartmouth, please come
and visit my house.
You will probably see me in my
bedroom window.
You can also join The Albert Mouse
Society

Albert

The Albert Mouse Trail

Now you can visit the places that appear in the
Albert Mouse books.

Just look for these blue stickers around
Dartmouth.

*By Appointment to
children's imagination*

If you have enjoyed this book, then please take a minute to leave a review at
www.jameshywel.com

You can also sign up for our blog to receive updates on new books from James Hywel.
https://jameshywel.com/blog

Thank you, I appreciate your support!

Acknowledgements

I'm grateful to Brian and Pam, the human owners of Cherub Cottage, for sharing their house with Albert and his family.

Thank you to the people of Dartmouth for welcoming me into their vibrant town which holds an abundance of charm and seafaring history.

As always I am grateful to "Walter" for sending me the breeze that moves the willows.

About James Hywel

James Hywel is a children's author and creator of both Mr Milliner and Albert Mouse.

He is a member of *The Royal Society of Literature* and *The Society of Authors*.

For more books and updates:

www.jameshywel.com

Printed in Great Britain
by Amazon